THE ESSENTIALISTS

shine

20 Secrets to a Happy Life

hinkler

CONTENTS

	Introduction	viii
01	**CLARITY**	001
02	**DECLUTTER**	009
03	**VALUES**	017
04	**GOALS**	025
05	**MINDSET**	033
06	**STRENGTHS**	041
07	**MOVE**	049
08	**EAT**	055
09	**SLEEP**	063
10	**SOLITUDE**	071
11	**BOUNDARIES**	077

12	**BREATHE**	085
13	**MINDFULNESS**	093
14	**JOURNAL**	101
15	**LEARN**	109
16	**GRATITUDE**	117
17	**JOY**	125
18	**TIME MANAGEMENT**	133
19	**HABITS**	139
20	**VISION**	147

About The Essentialists	155
List of Sources	158
Acknowledgements	158

First published in Australia by Penguin Random House Australia Pty Ltd 2017
This edition published by Hinkler Pty Ltd 2021
45–55 Fairchild Street
Heatherton Victoria 3202 Australia
www.hinkler.com

hinkler

Hinkler Pty Ltd

Text copyright © Shannah Kennedy and Lyndall Mitchell 2017
Cover and text design © Penguin Random House Australia Pty Ltd
All internal photography © Shutterstock.com except author photograph on
p. 154 by Susan Bradfield

All rights reserved. No part of this publication may be reproduced, stored
in a retrieval system, or transmitted in any way or by any means, electronic,
mechanical, photocopying, recording or otherwise, without the prior written
permission of the copyright holders.

ISBN: 978 1 8651 5550 0

Printed and bound in China

This dedication is for you the reader.
May you apply the life skills you discover
from within these pages to master what is essential
for you to live your most inspiring, authentic,
calm, confident life.

—

This book is also dedicated to our children,
Jack, Poppy, Mia and Grace.
You represent everything that is essential to us.

—

Our husbands, Michael and Scott,
thank you for your ever-present support
and wholehearted belief in our vision.

—

The Essentialists

INTRODUCTION

This handbook is your essential go-to resource and inspiration to use during the course of your life, no matter your age and gender, no matter how young or old. It is the simple book of essential, foundational and fundamental life and wellness skills that no one ever taught you at school. This book is for everyone on the planet, and as your guide it will support, help and inspire you to live a full and enriched life. When the skills are put into practice they will have a major impact on your pathway and, ultimately, your happiness.

We live in ever-changing times, and sometimes life can be tough. We're constantly pulled in different directions and can struggle to cope with the pressures we're put under by external factors and, most importantly, by ourselves. We live in a world of time famine, 'stuffocation' and addiction to entertainment rather than education. So it's time to get back to the basics and what is essential to us, and to eliminate some of the noise and distraction. It's time to start living on purpose again.

Each chapter is short, educational, enormously practical and truly inspiring. Each explains one life skill – what it is, why it is essential to master – and includes a practical how-to lesson. The ideas we share, while simple, are ultimately game-changing once you have the courage to act on them and make them a part of your daily habits. There are tips and exercises to develop your self-belief and to upskill, along with ideas on how to connect with the flourishing, inspired version of yourself so that you feel ready to embrace the things you love to do. It's time to wake up and live – to feel vibrant, inspired, happy and in control of your journey by focusing on these essential core fundamentals.

When you learn and apply these methods and techniques you are committing to making these essential skills into new daily habits. The reward will upgrade your life – you will come into your A-grade game and experience happiness at a much higher and more authentic level.

This is your life. Do what is essential for it to be your best.

CLARITY

01

KNOW YOUR WHY

Your why provides you with clarity, meaning and direction.

CLARITY IS SUCH A SIMPLE WORD, and such an essential part of motivation and inspiration in life. To know who you are, where you are going and how you want to get there lightens your load and brightens the journey. Clarity in life allows you to move from the passenger to the driver's seat, to take control and get excited about the road of opportunity ahead.

Leaders, game changers, outstanding communicators and authentically happy people are masters of self-connection, awareness and understanding the basics of their why. They are in touch with their purpose, cause or the beliefs that get them up and going every morning.

Get in touch to open up an incredible sense of **freedom** in life.

Get in touch with **what** you do.

Get in touch with **how** you do it.

Get in touch with **why** you do it.

Without clarity you can find yourself relying solely on others' opinions and approval and staying in your comfort zone instead of taking some well-thought-through risks to advance forward. You may find yourself being defensive and at the same time not fully open to accepting compliments and praise.

Touching base every day with essential powerful questions to keep you connected with your mindset, your heart space, your purpose and your ultra-inspired self is a habit worth cultivating. The answers lie within you and the means of seeking them out will build your self-esteem and cut through the fog in your mind and day-to-day living.

Once the answers are clear, you will be able to hear your own voice and find your unique pathway, not someone else's. You will be focused on bringing value to your life rather than comparing yourself with others and getting caught up in the world of distraction, procrastination and mindless, meaningless entertainment. Focus, inspiration, motivation, happiness, vision and a forward pathway will open up to allow you to find the inner calm and harmony that we need and crave. This clarity will allow you to give without resentment and to embrace each and every day.

Clarity starts with asking yourself the most powerful questions and thinking about them until your answers are clear. Vague questions with vague answers lead to vague results, and will end up with you feeling like you are just existing rather than grabbing life by the horns and launching into it with great intention. So, take a little time to drill down and find crystal-clear clarity on the basic foundations of You Inc. Higher quality, simple questions lead to better results and outcomes in life, both personally and professionally.

If you have a big and hearty understanding of your *why*, you will always figure out the *what* and the *how*. If you don't have clarity around your personal BIG *why*, you'll always use the *what* and the *how* as an excuse for not doing, living and being the absolute best and most thriving version of yourself.

To get you closer to your true self again, to connect with your own personal foundation, the core of who you are and what your life journey is about, start with asking yourself these simple yet powerful questions:

- What or who is most important to me?
- What do I want right now?
- Who and/or what inspires me?
- What made me happiest as a child?
- If I didn't have fear, what would I do moving forward?
- If I didn't have a job, what would I do with my day?
- What am I putting up with right now?
- What do I want my life to look like in three years' time? What mindset would serve me better moving forward?
- Where do I sabotage myself mentally, physically and emotionally?
- How do I want to be remembered?

'At the centre of your being you have the answer; you know who you are and you know what you want.'

— LAO TZU

Clarity will assist you to acquire the skill of being adaptable in life to whatever situation you find yourself in. It will guide you to make decisions that support you rather than sabotage you. Self-esteem is built on self-respect, integrity and authenticity, which come from a basic knowledge and connection with your mind, heart and body. Knowing the answers to the questions will always help you to feel your authentic self once again, to be at ease with yourself physically and to develop a healthy and positive attitude to life.

To have longevity in your career, relationships and wellbeing both personally and professionally, gain some clarity and master the ability to adapt to change without losing who you are.

DECLUTTER

LIVE

WITH

SIMPLICITY

Make space to be creative, spontaneous and free.

YOUR ENVIRONMENT SAYS A LOT about your state of confidence in life. Clean, open, soul-nourishing spaces give your body and mind room to breathe, grow and maintain perspective. Your surroundings significantly impact your attitudes, experience of life and happiness and can dictate the base level of stress you may experience each day. When you are in a simple, clean, organised and bright space you tap into your productive, motivated and more energetic self, which lifts life to new heights.

The art and mastery of the skill of simplicity is one of the most valuable and yet most underrated qualities you can strive for and embrace in life. Many of us live in a world of 'stuffocation', where our identity is defined by our belongings. Simplicity represents clarity, presence and freedom from effort. It allows you to clear your mind so you can continue on your journey with confidence, free from the clutter that's holding you back. In this state you open the gates of opportunity as you have a solid, basic, well-functioning structure and lifestyle that is adaptable to change.

The very idea of living an uncluttered and simplified life with less stuff immediately makes our minds feel less trapped. Owning far fewer possessions means there is less to worry about, look after, clean, organise and store. Most importantly, it will assist you with greater economic security and time to foster what you are most passionate about in life. You will experience real freedom to grow and be able to focus on your health and wellbeing, allowing you to create more experiences in your life and live more mindfully.

Clutter is stuck energy and is represented as a gradual build-up of items, new and old, precious and pointless. Your body also experiences clutter when it is filled with stuck and old thoughts, many of which sabotage your days and your goals. Tired, negative beliefs and habits create a low-lying level of weight and stress in your mind and body, which can be detrimental as we strive and grow from year to year.

'Life is really **SIMPLE**, but we insist on making it complicated.'

— CONFUCIUS

In today's world of consumerism we tend to ascribe too much meaning to our belongings, often at the price of our health, our relationships, growth, authentic experiences, passions, and our desire to contribute and give to others. This is not the formula for a happy and easy life.

When you realise that keeping your life simple, both internally and externally, is an essential skill, you will be able to relish a new-found sense of freedom and confidence. This results in having fewer worries and fewer things to look after, and a mind with more open space to create the life you want to live.

Top Tips **FOR SIMPLE LIVING**

- Clean as you go, using the one touch policy – don't move things, put them away.
- Prepare for tomorrow today – get things ready and organised the night before.
- Set up systems with reminders in your diary for keeping on top of your spaces and routines.
- Create as much natural light as possible.
- Use a clean well-structured diary to support you to stay on top of your daily commitments.
- Don't confuse intent with action!

Decluttering your life is a great step towards creating a simpler, more streamlined environment that will allow you the space to attract new opportunities and move you towards optimal wellbeing both personally and professionally. It is about creating a sense of ease in life. Clutter puts the mind and body in a state of dis-ease.

The decluttering journey can be fun, creative and incredibly rewarding when you gain clarity on what you want to create. By making small tweaks in your routine, you will clear out the energy drainers and allow opportunity to come in the door. Simple, easy living will open up a whole new energy and happiness in your life – you just need to start small and make a commitment towards change. Remember, you spend many, many years accumulating and collecting more and more things, so it may take a little time to make decisions on what to keep and what to remove. In the end, long-lasting happiness is not created by accumulating physical things, but by life's journey itself.

Some areas for you to consider decluttering and simple living:

- personal environment
- finances
- relationships
- wellbeing

Top Tips FOR DECLUTTERING

- Make a list and choose a day each month to clean out a room.
- Give yourself some structure and deadlines, decluttering one room at a time.
- Get some help from family and friends if it is too overwhelming to do on your own.
- Decide if the room needs a small tidy-up, a revamp or an overhaul.
- Examine what's in the room and cupboards; does it have meaning and purpose?
- Ask, 'Is it essential? Does it work? Will I use it? Who am I keeping it for? Does it bring joy?'
- File, throw away or donate your belongings.
- Enhance each space and make it work for you – is it simple and easy to manage?
- Make the space look great for you, bring in nature and keep things that make your heart sing.

Pay regular attention to the practice of keeping your life simple, organised and minimal. The goal of simple essentialist living is to do more in our daily lives with less worry. This means doing what is right for us in an easy and effortless way.

DECLUTTER

VALUES

03

SIMPLE

DAILY

ALIGNMENT

Your values are the essence of who you are.

VALUES ARE THE GATEWAY to your authentic self. Values form your thoughts, words and actions. They are the ideals and beliefs that you consider most important in life. It is important to note that everyone's values are different, hence really understanding your own is essential for calm, confident living.

Your values serve as a great foundation piece in life – when you base your daily actions around them they can keep your world simple and in alignment. Consciously identifying and living by your values is an essential skill to simplifying your life, minimising stress and anxiety, and opening up your most confident self.

Defining your values is the first major step to take in unlocking your key to success. Once you have identified them, they will act as your go-to point for positive decision-making in life. By letting your values guide and shape your priorities and reactions, you will make better decisions when opportunities arise, and these decisions will have the flow-on effect of leaving you more content, happy, confident and satisfied. Values are the base of your emotional intelligence – they influence your behaviour and serve as a navigator in all situations.

Your values are the things that matter most to you. They help you to see if a decision you are making is an opportunity or in fact just a distraction. They are your guide to living and enjoying life to its fullest, and they represent what you are all about. Unfortunately, most people coast through life without any kind of consideration of what is truly important to them. This means that for many, life is something that 'just happens' to them. Without values they are listless, trapped by the feeling that they are just 'existing', frustrated or simply not experiencing true happiness.

What CAN VALUES DO?

- Values help you find your purpose.
- Values guide your reactions in difficult situations.
- Values help you clear the clutter in your life.
- Values are a base for decision-making.
- Values guide you in choosing the right path.
- Values help cement your sense of self and increase your confidence.
- Values help increase your overall level of happiness and self-esteem.

Your core values are shaped by everything that has happened to you in your life and include influences from your parents and family, your religious affiliation, your friends and peers, your education, your reading, and more. Effective people recognise these fundamental influences and identify and develop a clear, concise and meaningful set of values/beliefs, and priorities, from them. Once identified and defined, values impact every aspect of your life.

For long-term success, your goals and life purpose need to be grounded in your values. When you live out of alignment with your values, or in 'values conflict', you may find that you are living without a sense of achievement or feeling a little out of control. By making a deliberate and conscious effort to identify and live according to your key values, you will minimise stress and anxiety in all areas of your life.

Knowledge of your own set of values offers you protection from the barrage of external influences and brings a great sense of empowerment. The process of understanding your values invites you to go within and cultivate an inner awareness of what is truly valuable to you. If you strip life back to its bare bones, you will see clearly what is fundamentally most important to you. You will discover an unwavering belief in what you stand for, and you can live a happier life doing what is important to you rather than living someone else's life.

Identify and consider whether or not you are living in alignment with your own set of values.

Choose the three values that are most important to you: the values you believe in and that define your character. Then live them visibly every day, both at work and at home. Living your values is one of the most powerful tools available to help you be the person you want to be, to accomplish your goals and dreams, and to lead and influence others. Don't waste your best opportunity.

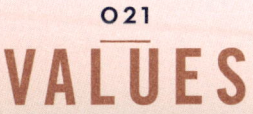

To get you started, here are some values that may resonate with you:

Family happiness	**Self-respect**	**Generosity**
quality time, bonding	sense of personal identity, pride	helping others, improving society
Competitiveness	**Recognition**	**Wisdom**
winning, taking risks	status, recognition from others	discovering and understanding knowledge
Friendship	**Advancement**	**Spirituality**
close relationships with others	career promotions	strong religious or spiritual beliefs
Affection	**Health**	**Loyalty**
love, caring	mental, physical	devotion, trustworthiness
Cooperation	**Responsibility**	**Culture**
working well with others, teamwork	being accountable for results	race or ethnicity identity
Adventure	**Fame**	**Inner harmony**
new challenges	public recognition	being at peace with oneself
Achievement	**Involvement**	**Order**
sense of accomplishment	belonging, being involved with others	stability, conformity and tranquillity

Wealth getting rich, making money	**Economic security** strong and consistent income streams	**Creativity** being imaginative, innovative
Energy vitality, vim, vigour	**Pleasure** fun, laughs, a leisurely lifestyle	**Integrity** honesty, sincerity, standing up for oneself
Freedom independence and autonomy	**Power** control, authority or influence over others	**Personal development** use of personal potential

Identify your values –

write them down –

act in alignment with them.

GOALS

04

MASTER

YOUR

FOCUS

Great goals motivate, inspire and assist you with prioritising life.

SETTING GOALS IS AN ESSENTIAL LIFE SKILL to master for a rewarding life. Goals bring a great sense of focus to your world, which is oversupplied with complicated opportunities and a plethora of distractions. When setting goals you are deciding what's next in life, so you can strategise how to get it. Goals initiate behaviours, and when you set simple goals with achievable time frames, accountability and support, you will be sure to succeed.

Goals help you clarify the tasks that will lead you to what you want to achieve in the world, and they provide a framework for smart choices and decision- making. They streamline and simplify your intentions, strip away worry and relieve you of the torment of choice. Writing down your goals is how you make things happen and gain traction in life. Having clear goals will not only give you a sense of purpose and direction, but will also increase your overall satisfaction and wellbeing.

Most people travel through life without bothering to write down their goals. Very few have specific and measurable goals, and even fewer have written them down. And only a fraction of these have thought of a specific plan to make their goals a reality. People who don't write down their goals are more likely to fail than those who have clear plans.

Setting goals is a skill that will deliver you incredible daily rewards. Having clearly defined goals also brings a greater sense of awareness and alerts you to new opportunities that will cross your path as you live in alignment with your values and visions. They will help you to stay on task as you work towards your vision and maintain your commitment and motivation. Your goals can engage and energise you and keep you on track with your mission, rather than living a life responding to your moods, other people and the parts of life you cannot control.

> '*Goals are DREAMS with deadlines.*'
>
> — DIANA SCHARF HUNT

Having simple, clear goals will help you measure your progress, which in turn will boost your motivation levels. Your confidence and self-esteem will also fire up as you achieve the goals you set for yourself.

It's common for people to complicate the goal-setting process. Your goals do not have to be big and bold life-changing feats. They can be as small as committing to taking three breaths before you get out of bed every morning and setting up your mindset for the day, or going for a walk every Saturday no matter what the weather serves up.

Often the small daily goals we set and act upon have the most powerful impact and offer the greatest reward over time as they become habits. We can also set big juicy goals such as starting a business, committing to a relationship, running a marathon, and break them down into bite-size plans within set time parameters.

Think about your ideal future and turn your vision into a reality.

Top Tips WHEN SETTING GOALS

- **Set goals with intention.** Really own them and have a strong and genuine desire to achieve them. For instance, you might make it non-negotiable to go to the gym at 6 a.m. on Monday, Wednesday and Friday with full commitment. The simplicity of the goal means no thinking is now required – you can just tick it off your list on those days as it's in the diary for the year.
- **Write down your goals.** Often said as, 'Don't think it, ink it', this is how we bring goals to life. Write them on paper, on a whiteboard, or type them if you have to. Make sure you can see them every single day: they are your road map to the vision you have created for your life. A study by psychology professor Dr Gail Matthews found that participants who wrote down their goals accomplished significantly more than those who simply thought about their goals. Written goals give you clarity and commitment.
- **Make sure they are specific goals.** This is the difference between the goal 'I want to lose weight' and 'I want to lose 5 kilos in five months'. Clarity makes it easy to plan how to achieve the goal and will start you in a mode of action.

- **Give yourself a deadline.** Ensure your timeline is achievable and marked in your diary. Simple effective planning of when you will do something equals incredible results.
- **Bite-size chunks.** Under each goal, write down the three bullet points that will back it up. For example, 'To lose 5 kilos in five months, I will go to the gym at 6 a.m. Monday, Wednesday and Friday; I will quit drinking sugar-laden soft drinks; I will commit to portion-sizing my meals to decrease my calorie intake.'
- **Evaluate daily.** What is not measured will never be mastered or finished. The most effective key to reviewing your goals is to reflect on them daily, even for just five minutes.
- **Reward your success.** Savour the moment when you get there. It will fuel you towards your next goal-setting endeavour.

The secret to accomplishing what matters most to you is committing to your goals in writing. Put them somewhere so you can see them daily, whether that's on the fridge, a mirror, the car's dash, at the front of your diary, next to your bed, in your wallet or as a daily reminder on your phone.

MINDSET

05

SET
YOUR
INTENTION

Step into the mindset you dream of living.

DID YOU KNOW that you may have on average 50,000 thoughts every day, and for years it was thought that the brain was fixed from birth without the capacity to change? In recent years, however, revolutionary research has discovered that we can create new pathways and train the brain. Training your mind takes a little effort and commitment, just like going to the gym. You don't go to the gym once and think you will be fit forever – similarly you don't do one mind-training activity and think that you will have positive, calm and confident thoughts forever. It requires a little more conscious effort to live this way, but the benefits far outweigh the effort in ways you may never have dreamed of.

By taking control of your thoughts you start to focus your attention in a directed way, and the result is you live a happier, more joyful life. Remember those moments when you felt like you were thriving, unstoppable and at the top of the mountain? What is similar about those occasions? Were you feeling confident? The brain and your thoughts are the control room to your happiness.

One of our favourite books is *Mindsets* by Carol Dweck, a psychologist at Stanford University. Carol researched the concept that there are generally two mindsets: a fixed or a growth mindset. Having a growth mindset means you believe your skills and intelligence are things that can be developed and improved. Having a fixed mindset means you believe that your skills and intelligence are set and can't be changed. Research shows that the growth mindset is what fosters grit, determination and work ethic in students, athletes and people of all ages. Carol Dweck's extensive research on the topic also reveals that people with a growth mindset learn, grow and achieve more and are happier than people who have fixed mindsets. Now that's a great train of thought to get on board!

It can be helpful to think of your brain as being similar to your computer. With your computer you have a program running and at any time you can update the program to help you work more efficiently and effortlessly. Crafting and evolving your own personal mindset program is about building connections to help rewire your brain to spend more time thinking positive thoughts that fill you with hope, faith, kindness, love and gratitude. The more frequently you travel the positive emotion pathways, the more often they become the freeway of choice for your thoughts. Then over time you will naturally experience more positivity and joy.

Having a positive mindset is a way of life, a way you choose to be. Elite performers know the importance of having a positive mindset for achieving iconic results. The same applies for everyday living. You can live in a mindset of fear and worry or you can choose to live in a mindset of faith and flourish. Positive people often have more confidence, live longer, have happier relationships and even reduce the likelihood of developing conditions like depression, hypertension and other stress-related disorders.

Having a positive mindset is not just a soft and fluffy feel-good term. Yes, it's great to simply be happy, but those moments of happiness are also critical for opening your mind and enabling you to explore and build skills that will be valuable in other areas of your life. Almost anybody in any situation can apply these lessons to their own life and increase their positive attitude. As you might imagine, positive thinking offers compounding returns, so the more often you practise it, the greater benefits you will realise. Schedule time for play and adventure so that you can experience contentment and joy while you explore and build new skills.

**Your time really is now: time to release all excuses, reasons, rationales and resentments.
Today is a fresh canvas. A new beginning.**

037
MINDSET

Top Tips FOR CREATING A POSITIVE MINDSET

— Start your day with a positive intention, statement or affirmation. Train your mind to allow the day to be terrific.

— Begin your conversations with a positive comment, reflection or action.

— Focus on the good things, no matter how small.

— Turn failures into powerful life lessons.

— Focus on the present, not on the past or the future.

— Use your phone to schedule daily mindset reminders, such as at 8 a.m. every day: 'Today is effortless and easy.'

— You are who you have lunch with, so surround yourself with inspiring light makers, game changers and people who enjoy life.

— Regularly ask yourself, 'Do I speak to myself (internally) the way I would speak to my closest friend?' If the language you use for yourself is different, reflect on what changes you could make to improve your thoughts.

Watch your thoughts,
they become **words**.

Watch your words,
they become **actions**.

Watch your actions,
they become **habits**.

Watch your habits,
they become your **character**.

Watch your character,
it becomes your **destiny**.

STRENGTHS

06

HARNESS

YOUR

POTENTIAL

WHEN YOU ARE IN THE STATE OF FLOW, whatever you are doing becomes effortless and more enjoyable. This is the state that athletes enter when they are at the peak of their game, that artists and musicians experience when they are lost in creating. In this state, nothing exists except the doing. Time stops. You lose all sense of self. You are challenged to the upper limit of your skill — but not beyond.

Today's positive psychologists agree that creating more flow experiences in your life is a definite way to push your positivity higher. Sonja Lyubomirsky, author of *The How of Happiness*, writes that flow is good for you because it is fulfilling, and the satisfaction you get from it is lasting and reinforces your confidence.

Your strengths are generally learned and shaped by your environment, your experiences and the values you identify with and choose to live by. We all have a collection of strengths that makes up our unique architecture, and getting to know our personal strengths is a way of unlocking the confident and competent part of us that thrives in high flow. For instance, if you love decorating, shopping for new outfits and changing around rooms, your strengths may be creativity, detail and a good appreciation for beauty. If you love going through new ideas with people, discussing plans and getting things done, your strengths may be relationships, planning and strategic thinking.

Numerous studies support the concept that identifying and living in alignment with your strengths can result in many benefits for your wellbeing and personal experience of life. Current research indicates that you are more likely to value a job, relationship, hobby or institution that aligns with your core signature strengths and allows you to regularly utilise them. In fact, finding new ways to use your strengths is one of the best ways to boost your long-term happiness.

Knowing your constellation of character strengths is the first step towards living a happier, more authentic life.

5 Reasons TO CONTEMPLATE YOUR STRENGTHS AND FIND OUT WHAT YOU ARE GOOD AT

---

1 — **Allows you to grow.** Sitting down and writing out what you are strong at, or what you can excel at, can help you reach higher than ever before. You can achieve so much more than you thought possible when you have clarity of vision.

2 — **Saves you time.** Finding out what you are good at will allow you to save time. The world needs all kinds of people with very different strengths. By focusing on what you're good at, you will set yourself up for long-term success instead of wasting time on having to relearn a new skill or job.

3 — **Boosts your self-confidence.** Identifying your strengths, no matter what they are, will give you a boost in self-confidence. When you feel confident, you can achieve so much more and live whole-heartedly.

4 — **Makes you a happier person.** When you feel good about yourself, you know you can do anything you set your mind to. Deep inside, knowing you have a skill set that gives you an edge will allow you to be a happier and more joyful person.

5 — **Allows you to be an inspiration for others.** When you have taken the time to analyse your strengths, you can use that knowledge to be an inspiration and a guide for others. By your example, you can be the light at the end of the tunnel for people who may be feeling lost.

Strengths AFFIRMATIONS

I have **faith** in myself and my abilities.

My strengths and talents will help me realise my **dreams**.

My **confidence** in myself increases daily.

STRENGTHS

'The energy of the mind is the ESSENCE of life.'

ARISTOTLE

4 Steps FOR STRENGTH ACTIVATION

1. Focus on your top three strengths. The best way to do this is to reflect on 'defining moments' in your career, relationships and life: times when you felt particularly engaged and inspired, and you were truly at your optimum.
2. Build new skills that draw on your strengths and will help you achieve your goals. If creativity is one of your strengths, how can you use this strength daily? Think outside the square for ways to tap into the skill set you already have.
3. Like most things in life, balance is optimum. Be aware that every strength has a shadow side when it is overplayed. For instance, judgement can be a wonderful strength to help you make the best decisions, but it can also be overplayed when you start to judge yourself and everyone around you more critically. Aim for balance in all your strengths.
4. When you are finding something challenging, think of your strengths and how you can use them to make the next step easier. Remember that most success is not built overnight.

MOVE

07

EXPERIENCE

OPTIMUM

WELLBEING

Find the movement recipe that is right for you.

MOVING YOUR BODY is your natural 'wonder drug'. Without movement we have no dance, no work, no play. Movement is fundamental and essential for optimal health and wellbeing, and changes both your inner and outer worlds. Moving encourages movement – the more you move, the better you move. Energy creates energy in a continuous, circling process – it is a constant dance.

We know that working out boosts our level of serotonin, the happy hormone. But the other benefits of exercise are also incredibly inspiring. Exercise causes an increase in various neurotransmitters such as adrenaline and dopamine, which are thought to have a positive effect on mood, and it helps you to switch off more easily. It is also thought to have benefits in improving memory, reasoning, attention and problem-solving. The stress-busting benefits of exercise also have a bolstering effect on the performance of our immune system and on our mental perspective in life. That's all in addition to a mountain of physical benefits such as weight management, increasing lean muscle, elevating your metabolism and increasing your energy and stamina.

We all know we need to do it. As human beings we benefit most from cardiovascular exercise and strength training to be healthy, fit, flexible and strong, with the healthiest heart and bones. That said, it's finding the recipe to your personal wonder workout that is the key to the sustainability and longevity of your bespoke exercise routine.

One size does not fit all when it comes to exercise and it is fortunate that we have such a diverse range of options available to us, from walking, cycling, swimming, rock climbing, dancing or running to yoga, tai chi or Pilates – forms of movement that combine muscle stretching with strength and flexibility. As we age our body changes and our exercise routine must evolve too.

The key to maintaining consistency with your exercise actually comes from adapting what you do to suit the needs of your body. For some of us exercise is all about the group environment – exercising or playing sport together. As individuals we have different reasons to join in the exercise tribe. The most important element is honouring what your own body thrives on and setting yourself up for the long term.

Setting a clear goal with your exercise routine can help to motivate you, because you have a measurable result to work towards, whether it's training for an event, to run a certain distance, or to develop a defined level of strength, flexibility or stamina. An exercise goal will motivate you when you feel a little flat by giving you the purpose and inspiration to get up and get moving.

At the end of the day, exercising is all about you and your body and finding what works best. Don't be afraid to enlist the help of a professional if you need a kickstart to make it happen or reach out to friends for accountability and motivation. Whether you want to exercise to unwind, make new friends, calm a busy mind or work towards your vision of an athletic, healthy body, exercise is a journey that empowers you and can be life changing. Remember that the one way to wellness is *your* way.

Top Tips TO GET YOU MOVING

- **Variety is key.** There are so many different ways to exercise. Be creative and find a way that is both challenging and enjoyable.
- **Time of day.** We all have different body clocks and constitutions so some of us will be best early in the morning before we start our day, while others will find the early evening a better time. Find out which time works best for you.
- **Be a realist.** Be realistic with the time you can devote to exercising, and avoid comparing your routine to others'. What works for others may only create frustration for you. Whatever works for you, do it. If it doesn't, find your own way.
- **Pain barrier.** Pain is the body's protective feedback system. While it is ok to push our usual limits when we are in optimum condition, beginners need to constantly evaluate the difference between discomfort and pain.
- **Ten minutes.** On those days when you just don't want to exercise, take the expectation off and simply commit to ten minutes of movement. Most times your endorphins will kick in and you'll be on your way. If not at least you gave it a go, and tomorrow is a new day.

EAT

08

REFUEL

YOUR

TANK

THERE IS NO single magic eating plan or formula, as everyone's body is different. No matter what your age, your daily food choices can make a huge difference to your overall health and in how you feel and look. Eating a healthy, balanced diet every day provides the nutrients your body needs to keep your bones, organs and muscles in optimum shape. Healthy eating can also help you maintain an optimum weight, boost your heart health, prevent diabetes and improve your brain function.

Healthy eating is a lifestyle choice, not a diet. Diets provide you with short-term gain, whereas leading a healthy lifestyle is for the long term and can change your life for the better. Quite simply, nutrition is essential for good health. It doesn't matter how much you exercise, if your diet is full of fast food, takeaways, pre-packaged meals and processed snacks, or foods that don't suit your body, you will struggle to truly nourish your body and give it the energy it needs to perform at its best.

A great place to begin is to start thinking of food as your fuel source and discovering what fuel works best for your body. If you want Formula One performance from your body, what should you be refuelling with? Once you have established what the best fuel source is for you, then you can focus on setting the structure to support this. It's easy to find excuses to skip meals, but if you are seriously committed to maintaining your health then you need to prioritise your nutrition.

Eat **seasonal**.

Eat **local**.

Eat **organic**.

Eat **wholefoods**.

# 4 Steps TO HEALTHY EATING

1 — **Consistency is key.** Setting and maintaining a routine with your meals is one of the most health-enhancing practices you can incorporate into your life. Your body thrives on routine, whether it's sleeping or digesting dinner. Keeping to a regular eating time aids digestion and helps to sustain your energy level throughout the day. Where possible, avoid having long gaps between meals and, ideally, eat a healthy snack every couple of hours to keep your blood sugar levels stable.

2 — **Eat seasonal produce.** When you eat seasonal produce you help to keep your body in sync with the season. Eating food during its natural harvest season in your region will help to bring your body into harmony with the ever-changing seasonal energies. When the weather is cold, foods with properties of warmth (citrus fruits, pears, root vegetables, broccoli, cauliflower, ginger and garlic) are ideal. And during summer you'll probably enjoy eating cooling foods (berries, watermelon, mangos, snow peas, zucchini, tomatoes, corn, basil, chives and coriander) that balance the heat of the season.

3 — **Eat when hungry.** Sometimes we eat because we're bored, lonely, sad, angry or because sheer habit tells us to put something in our mouth. Food can stretch beyond what is on your plate – healthy relationships, regular physical activity, a fulfilling career and a rich purposeful life can fill your soul and satisfy your hunger for life. Lack of emotional awareness is a trap for over-eating and bingeing. Be inspired by Don Juan's characteristic of the warrior, the person of power: the warrior will sleep when tired, rise when rested, and eat when hungry. Be mindful of when you are eating and listen to the triggers from your body.

4 — **Eat to de-stress.** What you eat has a profound effect on how efficiently your immune system performs. For instance, if you have been especially stressed and feel run down, increasing your intake of fresh, raw vegetables will be beneficial because of the antioxidant nutrients yellow, orange, red and dark green fruit and vegetables contain. Learning to identify the dietary ingredients that calm and soothe your mind, emotions and body will guide you to making better choices and tame the rollercoaster ride of emotions you may be experiencing.

10 Tips FOR ACHIEVING BUSY-PROOF, HEALTHY EATING

1 — Use smaller plates to avoid over-eating.
2 — Do a weekly meal plan to take out the daily thinking about what to eat.
3 — Feast at sunrise and fast at sunset by making breakfast your best meal.
4 — Resort to a nutrient-packed smoothie when lack of time interferes with your plans.
5 — Eat foods that suit your body and gut health.
6 — Reduce your sugar intake.
7 — Focus on eating right for life and avoid jumping from one diet to the next.
8 — Eat seasonal produce.
9 — Avoid foods that contain chemical preservatives to extend their shelf life.
10 — Make a weekly time to restock your freezer with healthy choices.

Healthy Eating AFFIRMATIONS

I choose to **nourish** my body.

Every day I feel a complete sense of **wellbeing**.

I live a **full and complete** life in body, mind and soul.

My **actions** support my health and wellbeing.

I am strong, happy and **healthy**.

SLEEP

09

RECHARGE YOUR BODY

Give yourself permission to rest and relax.

How you feel when you wake up says a lot about the night you had and the day to come. Sleep is without doubt a fundamental part of feeling healthy, confident and happy in life. We need good-quality sleep to recharge and re-energise our bodies every day.

It may seem harmless to knock out a few emails before bedtime, or flick through your social media, but by keeping your mind engaged technology can trick your brain into thinking it needs to stay awake. And if you're surfing the web, seeing something exciting on Facebook or reading a negative email, any of those experiences can make it hard to relax and settle into slumber.

After spending an entire day surrounded by technology, your mind needs time to unwind, gain some space and prepare for its nightly recovery process. Studies have shown that even your small electronic devices emit sufficient light to miscue the brain and promote wakefulness. As adults you are subject to these influences and so are your children.

The deepest and most regenerative sleep occurs in the first half of the night. During this time your body is designed to be in a state of rest, repair, rejuvenation and probable detoxification (elimination of waste products). This may mean you need to give yourself a bedtime curfew in order to create a consistent bedtime routine.

Where your focus goes, energy flows, and this also applies to sleep. We all know how great it feels to have a deep, restful night's sleep and also how death defying it can feel to have a night of sleep deprivation. For many people, a good night's sleep is the hallmark of optimal health.

Adequate sleep is a key part of a healthy lifestyle, and can benefit your heart, weight, digestion, memory, creativity, productivity and immune function. In a world crippled with insomnia, this is an essential skill to master.

'Sleep is that golden chain that ties health and our bodies together.'

THOMAS DEKKER

Yet we constantly push ourselves to get by on less and less until we don't even remember what 'peak performance' feels like. Treat your bedtime like an appointment – give it the same priority and importance you give to all your work-related appointments. It is, in effect, a meeting you have scheduled with yourself. And it's one of the best tank-toppers you can do, at no cost whatsoever.

We have two predominant hormones associated with sleep: serotonin and melatonin. Serotonin, the happy neurotransmitter, is key to having a good night's sleep. It has a relaxing effect on the body and, in unison with melatonin, helps to regulate our sleep cycle. The good news is that you can harness its power to help you drift off faster and sleep deeper.

As you start winding down and relaxing in bed, your serotonin levels increase. Serotonin is a precursor to melatonin, which helps stimulate sleepiness, lowers your body temperature and regulates your sleep cycle.

While the amount of sleep adults need varies from person to person, for the most part it is seven to nine hours a night. There are outliers, but that captures most people. The quality of sleep during that time is as important as the amount of time you spend sleeping.

4 Ways TO IMPROVE SLEEP

1 — **Tech curfews.** The majority of the screens we have come to love as a part of our lives, such as smartphones, monitors and tablets, also happen to emit a blue light that can create havoc with our sleep cycle. Disconnect with technology one hour before bedtime. No technology in the bedroom is an easy way to find more space in life.

2 — **Physical activity throughout the day.** Humans are not made for sitting, and sitting seems to be the new smoking. Being active during the day has a list of benefits as long as sleeping. Move your body, even if it is just taking the stairs at work or walking around the block after dinner. A little movement is better than none and helps the body to rest properly.

3 — **Eating curfews.** Make your night-time eating curfew two hours before going to bed so digesting your last meal or snack doesn't interfere with your sleep. As well as eating you could create a coffee curfew at lunchtime so the caffeine doesn't impact your sleep.

4 — **Download before bed.** Before going to bed make a list of everything that's on your mind, then finish with a gratitude list. This practice allows your mind to rest and makes gratitude your last waking thought. Better still, pick an affirmation from the list below to prepare your mind while you drift off into a peaceful, restorative, serene sleep.

Sleep AFFIRMATIONS

I have done my **best** for today.

I have earned my **rest** for tonight.

I have put my **love** into all my deeds.

I have used **kindness** in all my thoughts.

I close this day with **pure joy** and now drift into **sound sleep**.

SOLITUDE

10

MAKING

SPACE

ONE OF THE REASONS we don't take enough personal time is that it can make us feel guilty – guilty that we should be doing more around the home, that we should be doing more at work and that we should be doing more with the family, as well as exercising and eating well etc. Just like our never-ending to-do list, that feeling of doing more will not go away. Sure, there are always tasks and people we can invest more of our time, effort and energy in, but first of all we need to start with a solid base for ourselves.

In past generations it was a badge of honour to put yourself last on the priority list, but these days we know that placing yourself last leads to feeling drained, exhausted, frustrated and resentful. To be the best partner, role model, friend and employee you can be, you *must* find a way to refuel on a regular basis and take the guilt-free 'me' time you need.

Quiet time allows you to switch off, to turn down the noise, to self-reflect, to rest and repair; to be present, to notice, to find solutions. As you evolve and life becomes more complex, you can become more serious and too focused on work, forgoing any real alone time to pursue the hobbies and personal interests that spark your enthusiasm, passion and zeal. So often we tell the people dearest to us that we will be more present and loving when things slow down. We promise ourselves that we will get into peak physical condition and eat healthier food when we have a bit more time. Yet, deep within us, each one of us knows there will never be a better time than now to live our happiest, biggest life.

Switching off and having time for yourself is giving your body time to rest and engage in activities that inspire, engage and top up your tank. For some people this will start with giving yourself permission to simply stop and carve out a small amount of time in your diary. Enhancing your happiness and overall health starts with giving yourself permission to feel better, be better and become better. Self-care is an essential skill to master.

Embracing your need for quiet time is one of the greatest gifts you can give to yourself and to those around you. So gain some space, do something creative, get in the garden or focus on a hobby. Schedule the time for exercise. When you have the chance to enjoy quiet, peaceful moments and feel recharged, you are in a better position to be kind to others, care for your loved ones and make a difference in the world.

Silence is a source of GREAT strength.

— LAO TZU

3 Ways **TO CREATE GUILT-FREE SOLITUDE**

1. **Overcome old fears.** See solitude as a quiet and inspiring experience. Gather your courage and try something that you really want to do, something that stretches you to leave your comfort zone. Outside your comfort zone is where you will find your greatness.

2. **Let go of guilt.** Some people are invigorated by social interactions and external stimulation (extroverts). Other people are recharged by quiet time spent alone, which helps them feel ready to go back into the world with renewed energy (introverts). Both extroverts and introverts have their own unique strengths. So, if you fall on the introverted side of the spectrum and need time alone to recharge, why feel guilty about it? It is simply a part of who you are, so embrace and honour it.

3. **Change your mindset.** Instead of feeling that quiet time is a guilty pleasure, recognise that it is an essential part of self-care and replenishing your energy levels. Solitude can provide the restorative silence and serenity you need after a fast-paced, challenging day.

BOUNDARIES

11

PROTECT THE ASSET

PROTECT THE ASSET, which is you, by mastering the art of setting boundaries. Boundaries are essential to becoming a healthy adult and effectively balancing your work and personal life. They demonstrate your commitment to self-respect.

Personal boundaries are the physical, emotional and mental limits we establish to protect ourselves from being manipulated, used or violated by others and also from sabotaging ourselves. These boundaries allow you to separate who you are, and what you think and feel, from the thoughts and feelings of others. Learning to set personal boundaries is essential for communicating to others where your level of self-worth is.

One of the great benefits of setting the fences, or boundaries, around you, is that they will afford you the time, space and energy to devote yourself to what you are passionate about: your vision, dreams, goals and aspirations. Boundaries define where your responsibility begins and ends and clarify your needs in both personal and professional relationships.

Many people find it hard to set boundaries and end up with overwhelming feelings of resentment, frustration and misery because they have put everyone else's needs ahead of their own. The three main reasons why they have blocks around setting healthy personal boundaries are fear of rejection, guilt around letting others down and a misunderstanding of how to set effective boundaries.

Set personal boundaries and free yourself from the 'disease to please'.

There are many reasons why this incredible life skill is so important. Top of the list is that it defines who you are and is the base of your practice of self-care and self-respect. Another reason is that it allows you to communicate effectively and opens you up to the art of saying the gracious 'no'. And it can be used to set healthy limits in a relationship and give you time and space for nourishing emotions and interactions with others.

'This above ALL; to thine own self be true.'

WILLIAM SHAKESPEARE

Establishing boundaries that support you is an essential step to living the life you want. Boundaries will protect you physically, mentally and emotionally. They can be pictured as imaginary lines that help you keep other people's actions, behaviours and requests from hurting, distracting, annoying or imposing upon you. When you set personal boundaries that are in alignment with your vision, values and goals, you can also keep self-sabotage at bay.

Boundaries can be set in many different areas within your life:

- **Emotional** – being honest with yourself and nourishing your own energy
- **Mental** – owning your own thoughts and beliefs
- **Physical** – creating your environment, money, workplace, technology habits
- **Sexual** – having the right to say 'no' in a relationship
- **Social** – owning your time with all the roles and relationships you have in life
- **Spiritual** – protecting who you are, your values and your vision

Top Tips FOR SETTING BOUNDARIES

- **Know your limits.** Use the list on the previous page to help you clearly define your boundaries. Boundaries will become evident whenever uncomfortable thoughts or feelings arise. These are boundaries you have around other people, and also yourself in terms of exercise, food, money and environment.
- **Be assertive.** You might say, 'I'm sorry, I can't right now but will let you know when and if I can.' Or, 'I appreciate you asking me for help, but I'm stretched too thin right now to devote the time to be of quality help to you.'
- **Be firm.** If someone can't accept your 'no', then you know the person is probably not a true friend or doesn't respect you. Stick to what you believe in and don't compromise who you are for someone else's life journey.
- **Create space.** Set up technology curfews to create space for you to gather your thoughts and recover from the day's events. Take time to check your own schedule before shouting out 'yes' to everyone's requests of you. Unsubscribe to all the distraction coming into your life and create your non-negotiable list to protect yourself.

Life with boundaries doesn't mean being rigid or inflexible, but having good boundaries creates and cultivates a purposeful life with great meaning and happiness. It allows you to stay in the driver's seat.

Be blunt with your answer – do you suffer from wanting to please others at the expense of your own happiness? And if you do, what is the cost to your time, health, emotions and personal commitments? If something doesn't feel right, say 'no'.

> Be in **control** of your life.
>
> Be confident in your ability to say **'no'**.
>
> Communicate your thoughts and opinions with **confidence**.

BREATHE

12

MASTER YOUR CALM

That breath you just took... that's a gift.

BREATH IS ESSENTIAL TO LIFE. It is the first thing we do when we enter life and the last thing we do when we leave. In your lifetime you will take about half a billion breaths. What you may not realise is that the mind, body and breath are intimately connected and can influence each other. Our breathing is affected by our thoughts, and our thoughts and physiology can be influenced by our breath.

Breathing is essential for the function of your brain, nervous system and all internal organs. Oxygen is a vital nutrient that energises our bodies. We are all diligent at putting our phones on charge, but remember – every time you take a full breath you are recharging your body in the same way. Your breath has a powerful effect on your body and mind – and it's free. You can call on your breath at any time, it is your faithful friend; waiting there for you when you most need it.

Controlled, mindful breathing encourages relaxation and helps to cultivate the relaxation response. Many traditions like tai chi, qi gong and yoga have long focused on the power of the breath, and recognise it is the link between the mind and the body. Breathing deeply can help us deal with stress and soothe our nerves, as well as helping to lower our blood pressure and anxiety levels.

Breathing happens all day and night without conscious thought. It is our life force but we shouldn't take it for granted – if we can become more conscious of our breathing and master relaxation breathing strategies, we can take control of our health and wellbeing.

When negative emotions run high and your stress levels rise, your breath becomes short and shallow, utilising only about a third of your lung capacity. Fortunately, you can reclaim your physical and mental health by practising deep breathing exercises.

4 Benefits **OF DEEP BREATHING**

1. **Your muscles relax.** You'll find it becomes difficult to maintain a lot of physical tension in your body when you are taking deep, calming breaths.
2. **Oxygen delivery improves.** When you breathe deeply and you are relaxed, fresh oxygen pours into every cell in the body, with the effect of improving mental concentration and physical stamina.
3. **It helps to lower your blood pressure.** A common cause for high blood pressure is stress, so deep breathing exercises which help to reduce stress can also have a positive effect on your blood pressure.
4. **Endorphins are released.** Deep breathing triggers the release of endorphins, which improves feelings of wellbeing and provides pain relief.

These exercises can reverse your body's natural reaction to stressful conditions, which will help you manage negative emotions and even physical pain more effectively. We can't always eliminate stress from our lives, but we can learn to deal with it in a healthier way.

Breathing deeply doesn't have to be a chore and by being mindful of your breath you can easily make it an automatic habit just like brushing your teeth. There are some easy starting points to get you expanding your lungs, clearing your thoughts and settling your nervous system; experiment with the three-breath practice to get you started:

- When you wake up each morning, take three deep breaths before you get out of bed.
- When you get in the shower and enjoy the warmth of the water, take three deep breaths.
- When you turn on your computer and wait for it to start up, take three deep breaths.
- When you are sitting at traffic lights, try to push out the waist sash of the seat belt with your breath for three deep breaths.
- When you get on a plane, take three deep breaths.
- Before you go to sleep at night, take three deep breaths.

Integrating the three-breath practice into your daily routine will help reduce stress and enhance your clarity of thought. Deep breathing is a great way to stay calm and focused during the day. It's all about the small steps to success – one deep breath is better than none.

'For breath is life, and if you breathe well you will live long on Earth.'

SANSKRIT PROVERB

Here is a great starting routine that will help you learn the skill of deep breathing:

1. Lie down or sit in a comfortable position. Allow yourself to be free from distractions for one to five minutes.
2. Give yourself a moment to start relaxing your muscles. Become aware of any places that are holding tension and release them.
3. Counting slowly to five, inhale deeply, filling your lungs with air. Bring the air into your abdomen, not just your chest.
4. Counting slowly to five, exhale deeply, emptying your lungs completely. As you exhale, release tension from your muscles.
5. Continue to inhale and exhale deeply for a few minutes, counting slowly to five each time. Concentrate on your breathing and counting. Feel the calm in your body and mind.

A regular daily practice of deep breathing is one of the best tools for improving your health and wellbeing. Make it part of your daily routine and soon you will begin to breathe more effectively without even concentrating on it.

MINDFULNESS

13

SHARPEN

YOUR

AWARENESS

If you train yourself to become more aware of the ordinary, life can very quickly become extraordinary.

ANYONE CAN PRACTISE MINDFULNESS. It doesn't matter how old you are, what your physical ability is, or if you're religious. Mindfulness is not obscure or exotic; it's familiar to us because it's part of how we already are. We all have the capacity to be present, and with simple practice we can find many benefits.

Mindfulness is the simplest, clearest, purest train of thought you can have. It is capturing the ability and the discipline of noticing what you are doing, when you are doing it and becoming the master of your mind.

Mindfulness has evolved from the age-old Buddhist contemplative practice to an everyday life skill for calm confidence. The concept of mindfulness seems quite easy whereas the actual practice can be a little more challenging – but like all things, becomes easier over time. As Socrates so wisely said, 'learn and do, learn and do'. Over time your mindfulness practice can develop to be a part of daily living when you are walking, working, gardening, writing, cooking or just being.

When you were younger mindfulness came quite naturally – you only have to watch a toddler become absorbed with smelling the flowers or touching the grass to see it in practice. As you get older and have more to think about, staying in the moment becomes more difficult. Have you ever driven your car somewhere and arrived at your destination only to realise you remember nothing about your journey? Most of us have! Research shows that the average person is on autopilot 47 per cent of the time. Living this way, we often neglect to notice the beauty of life, because we are disconnected from what our bodies are telling us and are often stuck in old mindsets. On autopilot we tend to get lost in 'doing', so we find ourselves constantly striving and struggling and 'getting stuff done' instead of really living. It is our own distraction that robs us of the richness in life.

"There are only two ways to live your life. One is as though nothing is a miracle. The other is as though EVERYTHING is a miracle."

ALBERT EINSTEIN

Mindfulness is a form of meditation and what's great about it is that you can practise it any time, no matter what you're doing. Mindful eating, mindful walking, mindful working, mindful talking, mindful living – this is how you fill your confidence tank with golden moments in life. They are around you all day every day, and mostly free. While mindfulness is something we all naturally possess, it's more readily available to us when we practise on a daily basis. Whenever you bring awareness to what you're directly experiencing via your breath, your senses or your thoughts, you're being mindful.

Another powerful way to bring your attention into the moment is to focus on your five senses – sight, sound, touch, taste and smell. These are your gateways to the present moment.

The senses offer us a great place to start and to gain confidence with mastering mindfulness. They are available to us at any moment and they have the ability to instantly transport us back into the present moment. Remember that getting off focus is a part of life and the more we practise these basics the more we appreciate our wonderful lives.

MINDFULNESS

Sensory DELIGHTS

- tasting a good cup of coffee
- splashing your face with warm water
- listening to a child giggling
- relaxing as hot water from the shower hits your back
- smelling a delicious, rich meal in a slow cooker
- running your hands through a pet's fur
- breathing in the smell of freshly baked cakes or cookies
- admiring colourful flowers as they come into bloom
- putting on your old favourite jumper
- wrapping yourself in a soft blanket
- watching the ocean
- being woken by birds chirping in the early hours of the day
- taking a deep breath on a fresh summer's morning

Mindful AFFIRMATIONS

My meditation practice is my **daily gift** to myself.

I observe my thoughts **without judgement** of myself or others.

The more I develop my meditation skills, the more in touch with my **true self** I become.

MINDFULNESS

JOURNAL

14

CLARIFY YOUR THOUGHTS

Stop judging yourself and start seeing and connecting with who you are.

A JOURNAL IS A WRITTEN RECORD of your thoughts, experiences and observations. It allows your mind to process your thoughts at a deeper and more solution-focused level than just thinking. Journalling requires only a pen and paper, and doing this daily can upgrade your life. It is an incredible life skill to pick up and venture into.

Evidence and ground-breaking research on elite performance and ultra-achievement has revealed that keeping a journal on a regular basis boosts mental focus, increases self-confidence, elevates mental attitude and increases personal levels of happiness.

Journalling allows you to clarify your thoughts and feelings, which in turn gives you valuable self-knowledge. It is a helpful problem-solving tool as you can write about a problem and come up with solutions more readily on paper. Beyond keeping your creativity alive, writing regularly can give you a safe, cathartic release from the stress you may experience in daily life.

There are no rules around it, no right or wrong way to journal, which makes it a wonderful tool to use as a support structure in your life. Most people purchase a lovely notebook and pen and just get started, either in the morning or as a night-time ritual. Some will want to write a lot, while others may prefer to use bullet points, which are just as effective.

A strong foundation of self-worth will help you make the choices that are best for you.

'Journalling is like whispering to one's self and listening at the same time.'

BRAM STOKER, *DRACULA*

Benefits OF WRITING A REGULAR JOURNAL:

- boosts your level of happiness and confidence
- serves as an effective stress management tool
- deepens your level of self-awareness
- builds better habits as you acknowledge your actions and behaviours
- enhances your mood through gratitude
- heals your mind and body – journalling is an emotional release
- captures events in a safe environment where you can process them without fear or stress
- opens your mind to process and communicate complex ideas
- assists with harnessing your creativity
- builds your muscle of self-discipline – creating a domino effect for healthy habits
- sharpens your senses and evokes mindfulness by encouraging you to focus on the present
- increases your emotional intelligence
- boosts your IQ as you expand your language and ability to express yourself
- keeps you in touch and on task with your goals
- provides a way to record your wins, losses, learnings and moments to remember

JOURNAL

Top THOUGHT STARTERS FOR YOUR JOURNAL

- **Start writing about where you are in life at the moment.** Begin with your relationships, career, living environments, finances and mindset. Acknowledge what is real and connect with yourself.
- **Record your daily progress.** Consider small wins or achievements that boost your motivation levels and keep you inspired to grow. Explore what you saw, felt and experienced. Your life is grand and your journey is fascinating, so recording it, the people you meet and events that happen will motivate you moving forward. Journalling is a great reflection activity.
- **Write about your daily insights and learnings.** Jot down words, a conversation, a quote, events that happened, a book you read, podcasts or songs you discovered. Consider which of them you want to incorporate into your daily life going forward.
- **Cultivate gratitude.** Write a daily list of things you appreciate and notice – this will lift your mindset and boost your happiness. You might want to include your home, friends, family, health, food, nature, entertainment

or education. Rewire the negative with the positive through appreciation.
- **Dump your worry.** Clear your mind. Write about what is taking up your mind space. Creativity and growth require space, so declutter your mind by writing about your worries and what solutions could work to get you through.
- **Write your goals daily.** We live with dramatic distraction and are losing the art of focus and finishing what we started. Write down your list of goals each day to stay in tune, alert and on task with where you want to go.
- **Keep a log list.** List your favourite songs, movies, quotes, holidays. This list can lift you up when you experience anxiety, stress and lower moods.
- **Write what comes to mind.** Be free and just write. This could be about anything: ways you could nurture yourself, activities you like, questions you want the answer to, fears you are having, reasons to save money, jobs you aspire to, qualities you are proud of, things you value, ways you can help others, judgements you make or things to do when you are down.
- **Create positive endings.** End your journalling sessions with a few words about potential solutions to your problems, things you appreciate in your life, or things that give you hope.

LEARN

15

GROW,
EVOLVE,
FLOURISH

Education over entertainment will bring about your best possible life.

FROM THE MOMENT YOU ARE BORN to the moment you depart this world you never stop learning. Your dedication to this skill and its practice will allow your life to be enriched, nourished and greatly enhanced. Learning may not be in a traditional classroom setting, or even be a conscious decision – your daily life experiences will offer a great dose of teaching. But commitment to lifelong conscious learning is one of your most worthwhile processes as it will broaden your tastes, perspective, tolerance and understanding of the world.

The power of learning drives your personal change, growth, inspiration and motivation. Evidence shows there is a direct correlation between individuals who strive for growth and learning in their personal lives, and those who thrive in their professional lives, which is even more of an incentive to commit to the concept of lifelong learning.

Learning is when you gain a mental or physical grasp of a subject, when you take ownership of new knowledge and broaden your understanding of a topic. It involves thinking but also engages your whole being by involving your senses, feelings, beliefs, values, intuition and your willingness to grow. If you are not interested in learning, you will not learn. Learning as a skill depends not only on your ability but your motivation, personality, learning style and openness to want to develop as a person. It is an internal and intentional activity and one of the highest rated personal development tools.

A commitment to learning keeps your brain and mind expanding and more engaged, rather than just existing. Your mind needs stimulation for it to work at its optimal level, and by continually learning you can actually improve your brain function as you age. Learning will also assist you to deal positively with changes in life, as you are likely to require new tools and knowledge as you navigate through each decade.

Leaders are learners – the best in the world are full-time learners and committed to continual upskilling and education. Learning adds to the excitement of your life and assists you with making sense of the world.

The pursuit of knowledge is easier and more accessible than it has ever been. Advances in technology have opened up the world of knowledge and you can access and relay information online. But first and foremost you need to be willing to expand your mind and perhaps leave your comfort zone to take in new ideas that can expand your vision.

Top Reasons TO COMMIT TO CONSCIOUS LEARNING

- strengthen and enhance your skills
- stay up to date with technology
- stave off boredom
- increase confidence, resilience and social awareness
- increase your earnings in life
- grow your career, become a valuable asset
- become an expert in your field
- improve your brain fitness
- experience personal fulfilment
- positive role model for your children
- sustain hope and motivation in life
- increase your happiness
- gain a new perspective on life's ups and downs

How To LEARN

There are many simple, effective and realistic ways to implement daily learning opportunities that do not have to inconvenience your life.

To kickstart your learning, choose and focus on topics you are truly interested in and that will support your vision and goals.

- Set some learning goals.
- Commit to learning something new each month.
- Sign up to a course in a formal classroom.
- Attend lectures.
- Do some bite-size learning – TED talks, webinars, podcasts.
- Read all styles of books, both fiction and non-fiction, and join a book club.
- Read ebooks – they're great for reading when you're in transit.
- Take up writing – unlock and learn what your deep thoughts are and find clarity.
- Attend conferences to learn and network with like-minded people.
- Travel – it's an incredible form of education.

- Start writing a book and interview people to learn from them.
- Learn while driving, walking and resting. with audio books.
- Watch documentaries.
- Volunteer – share your time and skills while you learn.

Remember to keep an open mind and a liberal view on new creative opportunities for you to move forward.

LEARN

GRATITUDE

16

BEING

THANKFUL

Gratitude is like a healthy dose of vitamins for our relationships.

GRATITUDE IS AN EMOTIONAL STATE and also an essential attitude to embrace for a great life. Developing an 'attitude of gratitude' isn't just a fad or a new trend: it may be one of the most overlooked tools that we all have access to every day to thrive.

Gratitude can drive greater and deeper satisfaction in life when we induce and practise it daily. Cultivating gratitude doesn't cost any money and it certainly doesn't take much time, and the benefits are enormous. People who regularly practise gratitude by taking time to notice and reflect upon the things they are thankful for experience an increasing amount of positive emotions, feel more alive, sleep better, and express more compassion and kindness.

Feeling gratitude is one of the most beneficial ways to feel more inner harmony and peace. We can't control what happens around us or to us, but we can control how we react. Instead of becoming preoccupied with the future or worrying about the past, focus your attention on the present moment in all its richness. Rather than what you don't have, focus on what you do have. Martin Seligman, a leader in the field of positive psychology, defines gratitude as being aware of and thankful for the good things that happen. He considers it a strength that forges connection to the larger universe and provides meaning in our lives.

To be grateful sounds so simple, but there are biological reasons why this process doesn't come so easily to us. Humans are hardwired towards a negativity bias. This means we think about bad experiences for longer periods of time, focus on them longer, and they weigh more heavily upon us. In fact, researchers have found that our negative emotions have an impact close to three times stronger than our positive emotions. Our negativity bias had a strong evolutionary purpose: being highly attuned to danger in the environment allowed humans to survive natural threats. But those prehistoric times are long gone. The chances of us running into a sabre-toothed tiger on our way to work are slim to none, so it's time to wind down our negativity bias!

'When you realise there is nothing lacking, the whole world belongs to YOU.'

LAO TZU

These tips will help you minimise the effect the negativity bias has on your life and relationships.

- **Awareness** Be aware that your body is on guard with emotions of anxiety and fear. You are likely to react strongly to negative influences in your environment.
- **Be mindful** Allow yourself the time to stop and think about the whole picture before reacting to a given situation. When you face a negative event, make sure you take a deep breath before you react.
- **Savour** When something positive happens, pause and relish the feeling for several moments.
- **Self-compassion** Take care of yourself and your relationships. Provide yourself, and your family, with a variety of opportunities to experience the positive.
- **Positivity** Research reveals that negative experiences outweigh positive ones by three to one. Try to infuse your life with deliberate positivity.

Building an 'attitude of gratitude' is a simple way to improve your satisfaction and happiness in life.

10 Creative Ways
TO PRACTISE MORE GRATITUDE
---

1 — Notice and admire the beauty in nature each day.
2 — Make a gratitude jar – fill it with little handwritten notes from your day and watch your positivity grow.
3 — Write a letter to someone you've never properly thanked.
4 — Turn everything into a gift. Instead of your normal morning coffee, think of that cup as the gift of coffee. The gift of connection. The gift of laughter. The gift of a smile.
5 — Include a random act of kindness in your day.
6 — Smile more often.
7 — Commit to experiencing a complaint-free day.
8 — Say thank you for the little things people do for you.
9 — Enjoy the small things. With a minor task you do today, ask yourself how your life would be without it.
10 — Keep a gratitude journal – before you go to sleep, write down three things you are grateful for today.

Helpful Prompters **TO START YOUR GRATITUDE JOURNALLING**

Who do you appreciate?

What **material possessions** are you thankful for?

What **skills and abilities** are you grateful for?

What **surroundings** (home, office, neighbourhood, city) are you thankful for?

What **experiences** can you acknowledge?

What **opportunities** are you thankful for?

What **relationships** are you grateful for?

What are you taking for granted that you can **reconnect** with?

What have you **learned** today?

JOY

17

CREATE

THE

BLISS

JOY IS WHAT MAKES YOUR LIFE BEAUTIFUL. At the end of the day your happiness throughout life is what really matters. Joy, laughter, love and happiness are states of mind and orientations of the heart. Joy is a feeling of confidence, lightness, contentment and hope. Creating the bliss in your life is an essential skill and habit to ensure you are able to experience life with your heart full.

You are often taught to put your work first and the rewards will come later. You wait for the desserts in life, for the day to use or wear your 'good' things and wait for everything to be perfect before you allow yourself to experience joy. But often the result of this approach is stress, burnout, exhaustion and misery.

People can confuse self-care with selfishness. You cannot be the best most vibrant, generous version of yourself if your heart isn't full, your motivation bubbling and your resentment at bay. Focusing on your joy and creating the bliss in your life will fill your heart and allow you to be of higher service, open to more opportunities and enrich your daily life with lightness.

Whole-hearted joy is a sustained, conscious, elevated vibrating energy that can be harnessed when you understand what your recipe for it is. It will reveal eagerness and enthusiasm for life and take your motivation and inspiration to a new level. To find this place of bliss you need to focus on acquiring the skill of it, and building your capacity for intense, sustained and positive energy, bringing it to yourself and others. It does not come from a shop, it is cultivated and it is who you are at your deepest core.

How To MAKE HAPPINESS AND JOY A DAILY HABIT

- **Maximise your breath** – one of the simplest ways to control your mood.
- **Move your body** – to improve your perspective and motivation in life.
- **Do what you love** – cultivate more activity around what you love doing.
- **Find your tribe** – those people who bring out the best in you.
- **Practise gratitude** – focus on what is good in your life.

'Get interested in something. Shake yourself awake. Develop a hobby. Let the winds of enthusiasm sweep through you. Live today with gusto.'

— DALE CARNEGIE

3 Ways TO CULTIVATE BLISS

1 — **Daily rituals.** Create bliss points each and every day for yourself. The small commitments to your own joy and happiness accumulate and fuel your mind with positivity. Start building some joy into your to-do list each day. Speak with friends, go to that yoga or boxing class, indulge in a bath, turn off your phone and read a book, create some space, book a massage, write your journal, tidy up, get organised and be kind to yourself.

2 — **Hobbies.** Finding time for yourself is said to be the key to your own sanity. Having a hobby can improve all other aspects of your life, relieve stress, be a creative outlet and is a great way to meet new people. A hobby is simply anything you do that is fun for you and is not your job. It is done in your free time and will help you decompress, and it can connect you with other people or allow you to delve into your own self-connection. Creative hobbies, or side projects, help you tap into a sense of play and cultivate improvement in the thinking part of your brain. They allow you to do something that is just for you, that will help you unwind and give you pleasure.

Having an outlet that challenges and engages you can open up new ways of thinking, relieve stress, connect you to others and bring bliss into your life. Some examples of highly successful people who invested in the skill of joy are the late Steve Jobs, who discovered calligraphy; Phil Libin, the Evernote CEO who plays piano for an hour a day; and singer/songwriter Joni Mitchell, who paints for joy.

- Look to your past and what made your heart sing as a child – did you love riding your bike, painting, playing music, baking, playing outside?
- Solo or social – do you need alone time, or do you want to connect with others?
- Understand your budget – some hobbies are expensive, while others are free.
- Enlist help from friends – get introduced to a book club or do some classes together.
- Try again – keep opening up to the new, and never give up if you are not great at it first off.

Hobby ideas

- painting or drawing
- book club
- photography
- baking & cookery
- sports
- foreign languages
- dance
- exercise
- travel
- DIY projects

3 — **Bucket list.** By definition, a bucket list is a list of goals, things and experiences you want to do or try before you die. It provides direction, inspiration and motivation by opening your mind to opportunities and dreams that can cultivate joy and happiness in your life. Writing a bucket list can make you stop and think about what you actually want to experience in your lifetime and give you hope and curiosity.

- Dreamstorm – write down freely what comes to mind with no limitations.
- Get inspiration – research other people's bucket lists.
- Timeline it – break it into 20s/30s/40s/50s/60s/70s/80s lists.
- Share your list – create interest and buy-in to make it happen with a bucket list buddy.
- Get your top three ready to go – start planning who, when, where and how.
- Celebrate – blog it, share it, put it on your board, inspire others.

TIME MANAGEMENT

18

BE

THE

DRIVER

Open the door to more space, more sleep and more time for yourself.

MANAGE YOUR TIME and you will master your life. Time management is the process of planning and exercising conscious control over the amount of time you spend on specific activities – especially to increase effectiveness, efficiency or productivity. How you spend your hours and your days is a reflection of how you are spending and feeling about your life.

In this world of ever-increasing distraction, research suggests that during any typical day the average person at work is spending 2.1 hours in distraction, is interrupted every 11 minutes and takes 25 minutes to refocus their mind on the work they were doing before they were distracted. We all answer the question, 'How are you?' with, 'Busy, really busy'. Often, though, we are spinning our wheels and not really accomplishing anything on our to-do list or achieving the goals that contribute to our vision for a great life.

Being busy is not a badge of honour. Time management and the art of focus is fast becoming an essential skill to enable you to work smarter rather than harder. Time is the most valuable resource in achieving your A-grade life. There are only three ways to spend your time: in thoughts, conversations and actions. Regardless of the type of business you are in, or the lifestyle you have, your work will be composed of those three items.

Failing to manage our precious amount of time each day results in increased stress levels, anxiety, the release of the cortisol hormone in the body, a feeling of dissatisfaction and frustration, and a less rewarding life. It leaves us without energy to engage in and enjoy what we deem most important to us: our health, wellbeing, relationships and personal space.

We all have the same amount of time each day: 24 hours, 72 blocks of 20 minutes, or 1440 minutes. So what are you doing with your time, and is it working for you?

Most people have the mindset that we live in a time famine – there are not enough hours to get everything done because we have overcommitted and over-scheduled our time. In a world of chaos, you need to refocus on what matters most, realign your days with your top priorities and live by your highest intentions.

Powerful planning is the key to effective time management, achieving a sense of freedom and seeing great results. Structure is essential, just as it is in building a house – the foundations have to be measured and a plan drawn up with a timeline attached. Putting pen to paper will help you prioritise and achieve your goals easily and effortlessly. A powerful plan and mastering the skill of time management will allow you to go through life with great confidence and a heightened sense of wellbeing.

Remember, the quality of your life is determined by the choices you make each day. Sometimes you need to say no to the good things to make way for the great things you have planned and committed to for a truly rewarding and authentic life.

Super-Charged Strategies to Master Time

- Start your day with clear focus and purpose.
- Have a dynamic and prioritised task list.
- Outsource and delegate what you can to free up time for your big-ticket items.
- Make intentional compromises when necessary, as people do come first.
- Focus on your highest value activities that are essential to achieve your goals.
- Minimise your interruptions and get real on your perfection expectations.
- Do the hardest thing in the day first and put a stop to procrastination – just do it.
- Limit your multi-tasking as it kills effectiveness and focus.
- Review your day, and celebrate and prepare for the following day.

TIME MANAGEMENT

HABITS

19

HARNESS

YOUR

POTENTIAL

HABITS ARE THE CORNERSTONE of day-to-day living. For better or for worse, your habits shape you, and your life to date is the sum of your habits. A good habit can be a strong ally in your pathway to becoming the person you want to be, while a bad habit can act like a weight on your shoulders and sabotage your best intentions. Mastering your habits to support your vision and goals will change your life.

Have you ever wondered why 3 p.m. rolls around and you find yourself on autopilot devouring a choc chip cookie that you promised yourself you wouldn't eat today? It is good to know that this is normal and natural behaviour, a habit you have developed, just like brushing your teeth or using your computer. These behaviours, whether good or bad, become hardwired pathways in the brain. The good news is that it's not too late to reverse your bad habits and start living a happier, healthier life.

Habits emerge because the brain is constantly looking for ways to save effort. Forty per cent of the actions people perform every day are not actual decisions but rather habits. Researchers at the Massachusetts Institute of Technology discovered a simple neurological loop at the core of every habit, a loop that consists of three parts: a cue, a routine and a reward. Just like your recipe for life balance, every person has a different recipe for changing habits and this loop provides a framework for understanding how habits work and a guide to experimenting with how they might change them.

The Habit LOOP

1. First there is a cue, a trigger that tells your brain to go into automatic mode and directs which habit to use.
2. Then there is the routine, which can be physical or mental or emotional.
3. Finally, there is a reward, which helps your brain figure out if this particular loop is worth remembering for the future.

Over time, this loop of cue–routine–reward becomes more and more automatic. The cue and reward become intertwined until a powerful sense of anticipation and craving emerges.

'Motivation is what gets you started. Habit is what keeps you going.'

JIM ROHN

When a habit is formed, the brain stops fully participating in any decision-making. So, unless you deliberately fight a habit by finding new routines, the pattern will continue to unfold automatically. Habits are encoded into the structures of your brain so they never really disappear, but we can choose our habits if we understand how they function. Once you understand that habits can change, you have the freedom, and the responsibility, to remake them.

Now that we understand the habit loop, the next step is deciding when to start your new habit. To give your new habit the highest chance of success, schedule it in the morning. Where possible, we tend to organise work that requires high concentration and brainpower in the mornings, when our self-regulation is at its highest. As we work through the day our self-regulation peters out, which gives reason to the 3 p.m. pick-me-up or the excuses for not exercising at the end of the day. And finally, remember that your brain likes novelty, so every now and again change it up and vary the rewards. By doing that you will get another boost of inspiration to propel your habit forward.

You can gain a lot of insight into your habits by answering these five questions:

1 — Where are you?
2 — What time is it?
3 — What's your emotional state?
4 — Who else is around?
5 — What action preceded the urge?

Write down the answers to these five questions every time you experience a habit cue, and you will take that first step towards making a lasting change. Then simply ask yourself:

What is the **bad habit** I would like to change?

What is the **trigger** for this habit?

What is the **good habit** that I would like to embed to move forward in my routine?

Golden Rules OF CHANGING HABITS

- Don't resist craving – redirect it.
- To end a bad habit, replace it with a new routine.
- Replace the reward to avoid feeling frustrated.
- Cravings can also work to reinforce good habits.
- Small wins are important because they build motivation.
- You can't 'think' your way into a new habit. You must take action.
- All habits form a cue-routine-reward loop.

VISION

20

YOUR

LIFE

PLAN

Where are your goals going if you have no vision or path for them?

YOUR **PERSONAL VISION** is your roadmap for the future. It can be a very powerful and motivating force packed with purpose, in alignment with your values and intentions, and can inspire you to grow, evolve and flourish each year. For long-term success, the skills of vision creation and life planning are essential.

A vision is not just a picture of what you could be, it is also an appeal, a shout-out to your better self, a call to become something more in life. It gives you permission to dare to dream and create your future map.

A strong healthy vision and life plan, based on your values, will drive your decisions, goals and actions, and serve up a great dose of confidence in the process. Your vision will allow you to gain clarity on where you want to go in life, inspire and motivate you to make the most of each chapter in your life and refuel you with incredible rewards. The price of having no plan or no vision is feeling like you are stagnating – not moving, not growing, frustrated, stuck on the old treadmill, doing the same old things while watching others excel in life.

The clearer the vision, the more likely you are to stay on course and achieve the goals you set for yourself. With the distractions you live with day to day it's easy to become sidetracked and lose the art of focus on the essential tasks that will make you successful. The goals you set act like signposts on the way to your vision.

Developing a vision for yourself will motivate you to uncover and work on reaching your potential, opening yourself to opportunities and igniting a fire within you. You will be able to gain a greater perspective as you look up, broaden your mind and get out of the day-to-day monotony. A vision will give your mind a plan, a pathway, some destinations to get to, some big-ticket items to achieve and serve as another decision-making tool to support you in life.

To start the creation of your life plan, your vision for your best future, be bold and let your imagination decide what it wants most in life so you can plan how to get there. Many people start with a three-year plan then develop a five-year one, then a ten-year. You can create a vision board filled with images that appeal to your visual and creative side, or you can pick up a pen and write paragraphs describing your life vision. A combination of both is the most inspiring and achieves the best results.

Write down what comes to your mind without being held back by fears and self-sabotaging thoughts. Imagine you are not limited by lack of money, appropriate skills or shortage of time. This is your list of hopes and dreams, and how you want to feel in the future. Answering questions is the most effective way to deepen your thought process on any topic.

Powerful THOUGHT STARTERS FOR YOUR THREE-YEAR VISION

- How old will you be in three years' time? Write this at the top of your page.
- What are your values?
- What is most important to you?
- How would you like to be described by your friends, co-workers and family?

- Who inspires you and why? Who are your role models and mentors?
- What life experiences do you want to have?
- How much money are you earning and what are you doing with it?
- How fit, strong, flexible do you want to be?
- Where do you want to travel in this time?
- What makes you smile or brings you delight?
- What do you like about yourself?
- What hardships have you overcome?
- What do you really want for your future?
- Who do you need permission from to start taking responsibility?
- What kind of work will you be doing? How do you feel about this work?
- What's your health like? How are you getting these outcomes?
- Who brings you joy in your life? How do you spend your time together?
- What are you learning? What difference is this making in your life?
- What do you do for fun? Do you have a hobby or a passion project?
- Where are you living? What makes this feel like a haven?
- What have you conquered emotionally?

'Vision without action is a daydream. Action without vision is a nightmare.'

JAPANESE PROVERB

Your VISION BOARD

A vision board is a visual representation of how you would like your life to look. It assists you with purpose, clarity, direction and confidence as you review it to check your progress. Cut out pictures for your board or use Pinterest to create a life map. Use words, pictures of places you would like to travel, your fit and healthy body, your business goals, inspirational quotes, pictures of friends and family, living spaces, cars, activities you want to try – whatever will appeal to your inspirational future self.

Creativity and visualisation are life skills that can be practised. Your vision essay and vision board need to be compelling, exciting and inspirational. Write your three-year vision in the present tense so it excites and conveys your emotion and passion for your life. The clearer the pictures and the words, the easier it is for you to set goals, open up to opportunity and grow moving forward. Make sure you look at the words and the vision board each day for clarity, focus and inspiration. Let the excitement begin and the life plan support you!

About THE ESSENTIALISTS

Our Mission

The Essentialists work to engage, educate and empower individuals, teams and organisations with essential life and wellness skills.

The Essentialists help people take control of their health, wellbeing and ultimately their happiness by committing to what it essential in both their personal and professional life through the mastery of fundamental life and wellness skills. Our commitment is to equip people with skills to make the best, wisest and most authentic investment of their time and energy in their one and only precious life.

The Essentialists' way isn't about doing more, it's about doing what's right for you, wherever you are, in life's journey. This clarity allows for far more effective work and self-care practices that ultimately lead to breakthroughs in work and life. Better leadership, human connections, self-care, gratitude, empathy and joy in the every day. The results of The Essentialist programs are testimony to this.

Who Are THE ESSENTIALISTS?

Shannah Kennedy and Lyndall Mitchell
Educators of Life and Wellness skills

Together and as individuals, Shannah and Lyndall are acknowledged as Australia's leaders in life and wellness education. They combine more than three decades of teaching, presenting and executive coaching experience across public and corporate sectors globally. Their book *Chaos to Calm: Take Control with Confidence* has assisted many people create extraordinary lives.

They facilitate high impact wellness programs and life coaching and challenge their clients to question the pursuit of 'success' at all costs. Clarity on what is essential is key as they live and breathe by this mantra.

By coming together, Shannah and Lyndall offer a wealth of experience, complementary expertise and approaches to maximise impact for their clients globally. As working mothers, juggling family with thriving businesses, and a non-negotiable stance to their own health and wellbeing, commitment to basic fundamental life skills ensures they stay on track and thrive in the journey of life.

'We work to give you the skills and knowledge to transform the way you live and work, to eliminate the distractions and drainers, understand the value of self-care and get back to the essentials.'

Shannah and *Lyndall*

To book The Essentialists to speak at your next conference or discover more of their ideas, visit www.theessentialists.com.au

LIST OF SOURCES

- Dominican.edu. (2017). *Study demonstrates that writing goals enhances goal achievement — Dominican University of California.* [online] Available at: http://www.dominican.edu/dominicannews/study-demonstrates-that-writing-goals-enhances-goal-achievement [Accessed 14 Jul. 2017].
- Dweck, Carol S. *Mindset.* 1st ed. New York: Ballantine Books, 2008. Print.
- Lyubomirsky, Sonja. *The How of Happiness.* 1st ed. New York: Penguin Books, 2008. Print.

ACKNOWLEDGEMENTS

We express our deep appreciation to the entire team at Penguin Random House who support and believe in our passion to educate the world with essential life and wellness skills.

To our readers and clients who constantly fuel our fire and show gratitude for this incredibly important educational and inspirational work: you keep us fully committed to doing what is essential for us to thrive and live our best lives.